MATH

the

EASY WAY

Jason Winn

MATH THE EASY WAY

iUniverse books may be ordered through booksellers or by contacting:

iUniverse
1663 Liberty Drive
Bloomington, IN 47403
www.iuniverse.com
844-349-9409

ISBN: 978-1-6632-3985-3 (sc)
ISBN: 978-1-6632-3986-0 (e)

Library of Congress Control Number: 2022909203

Print information available on the last page.

iUniverse rev. date: 09/14/2022

Acknowledgements
To all this book will help.

Dedications
Sydney Winn and Cynthia Winn - outstanding people

How to MULTIPLY using the shapes...

- ☑ Draw the shape under the largest number
- ☑ Draw the dots on each side of the shape
- ☑ Add or count all the dots
- ☑ Write the answer

EQUAL MEANS "THE SAME"

$$4\text{x}3 = \begin{array}{r} 3 \\ 3 \\ 3 \\ \underline{+3} \end{array}$$

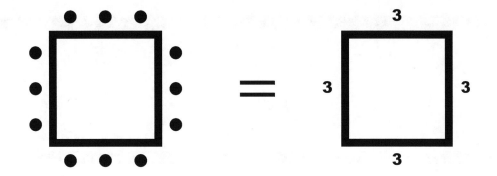

EXAMPLE PAGE

$$3 \times \boxed{} =$$

$$3 + 3 + 3 + 3 =$$

12

How to DIVIDE
using the shapes...

☑ Draw the shape under the smallest number

☑ Mostly, the answer is a multiple

☑ Each side has the same number of dots

☑ Write the answer

EXAMPLE PAGE

12 ÷ 4 =

3 + 3 + 3 + 3 =

12 ÷ 4 = 3

CHAPTER 0   "ZERO"

- ☑ Represents Nothing
- ☑ Can Decrease
- ☑ Can Increase
- ☑ Donut / Circle Shape

(1) "0" multiplied by a number is "0".

(2) "0" divided by a number is "0".

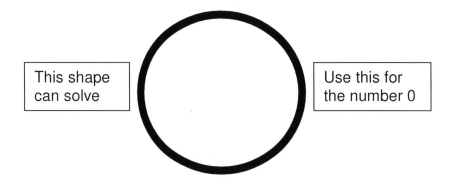

| This shape can solve | | Use this for the number 0 |

(3) "0" placed to the right besides the number increases the number.

(4) 10 = ten   100 = one hundred

CHAPTER 1 "ONE"

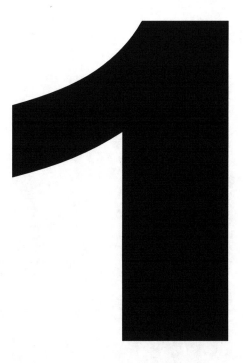

☑ Means ONE

☑ First number

☑ Single / Solo

☑ Alone

(1) "1" multiplied by any number is any number

(2) 1 x 1 = 1   1 x 2 = 2

This shape can solve

Use this for the number 1

(3) A number divided by itself is "1"

(4) 1 ÷ 1 = 1   2 ÷ 2 = 1

CHAPTER 2   "TWO"

☑ Means TWO

☑ Second number

☑ Duo / Twin

☑ Dual

(1)   2 x 2 =   2 x 3 =

(2)

This shape can solve

Use this for the number 2

(3)   4 ÷ 2 =   6 ÷ 2 =

(4)

CHAPTER 3 "THREE"

☑ Means THREE

☑ Third number

☑ Thrice / Triplet

☑ TRIANGLE

(1)   3 x 3 =   3 x 4 =

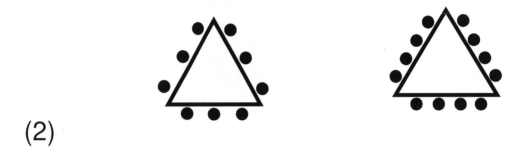

(2)

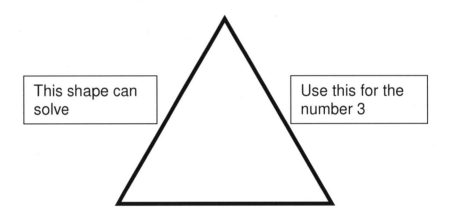

This shape can solve

Use this for the number 3

(3)   9 ÷ 3 =   12 ÷ 3 =

(4)

CHAPTER 4   "FOUR"

- ☑ Means FOUR
- ☑ Fourth number
- ☑ SQUARE
- ☑ "Best four out of seven"

(1)   4 x 4 =   4 x 5 =

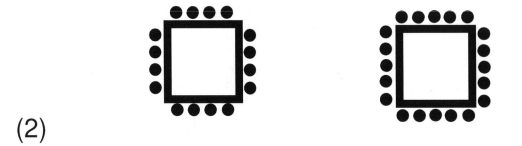

(2)

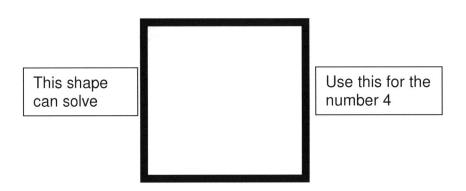

This shape can solve

Use this for the number 4

(3)   16 ÷ 4 =   20 ÷ 4 =

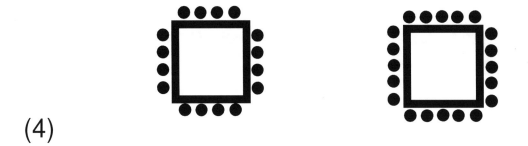

(4)

CHAPTER 5 "FIVE"

☑ Means FIVE

☑ Fifth number

☑ PENTAGON

☑ Looks like a house

(1)   5 x 5 =   5 x 6 =

(2)

This shape can solve | Use this for the number 5

(3)   25 ÷ 5 =   30 ÷ 5 =

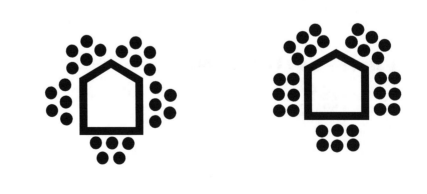

(4)

CHAPTER 6 "SIX"

☑ Means SIX

☑ Sixth number

☑ HEXAGON

☑ Honeycomb

EQUAL MEANS "THE SAME"

---

(1)   **6 x 6 = 36**   **-OR-**

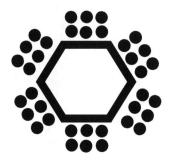

(2)

---

(3)   **6 + 6 + 6 + 6 + 6 + 6 = 36**

(4)

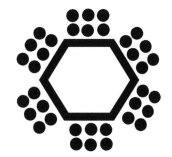

(1)   6 x 6 =   6 x 7 =

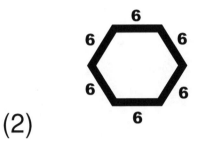 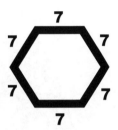

(2)

This shape can solve | Use this for the number 6

(3)   36 ÷ 6 =   42 ÷ 6 =

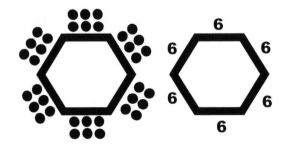 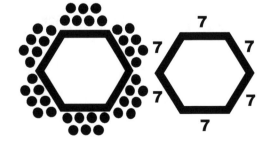

(4)

CHAPTER 7 "SEVEN"

- ☑ Means SEVEN
- ☑ SEVENTH number
- ☑ SEPTAGON, HEXAGON, ARROW
- ☑ ARROW, "World Series"

(1)　7 x 7 =　　　　7 x 8 =

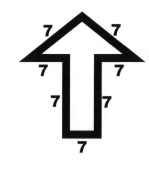 

(2)

| This shape can solve | Use this for the number 7 |

(3)　49 ÷ 7 =　　　　56 ÷ 7 =

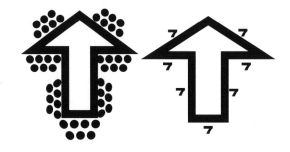  

(4)

CHAPTER "EIGHT"

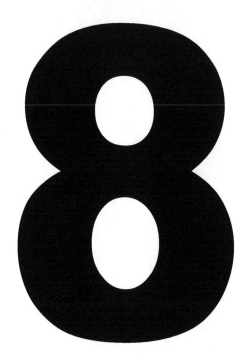

☑ Means EIGHT

☑ EIGHTH number

☑ OCTOGON, ARROW

☑ Stop Sign

(1)   8 x 8 =   8 x 9 =

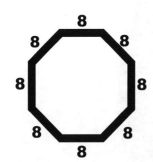 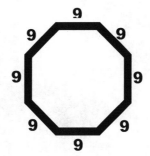

(2)

This shape can solve | Use this for the number 8

(3)   64 ÷ 8 =   72 ÷ 8 =

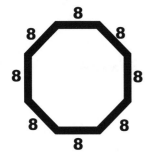 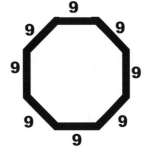

(4)

CHAPTER "NINE"

- ☑ Means NINE
- ☑ NINTH number
- ☑ Dreidel / Top outline
- ☑ Nonagon / Nine Sides

(1) 9 x 8 =   9 x 9 =

(2)

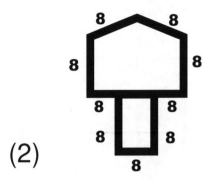 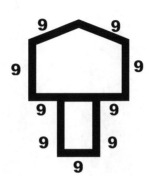

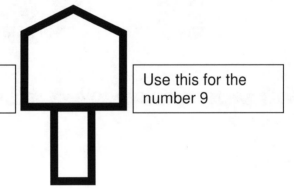

This shape can solve

Use this for the number 9

(3) 72 ÷ 9 =   81 ÷ 9 =

(4)

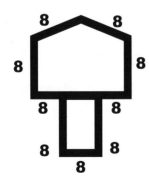 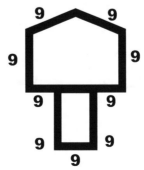

CHAPTER "TEN"

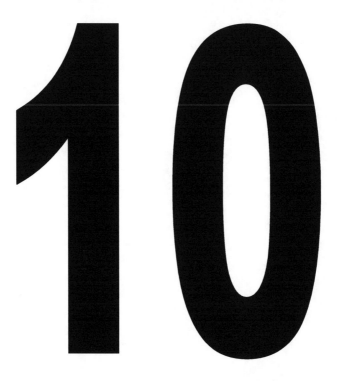

☑ Means TEN

☑ Decagon

☑ Ten Sides / Ten Endpoints

☑ "Decade"

(1) 10 x 5 =   10 x 9 =

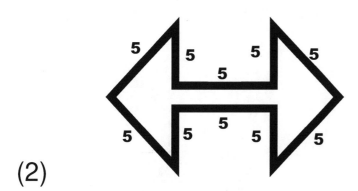
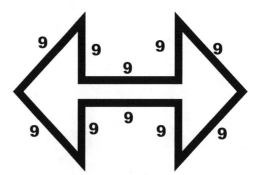

(2)

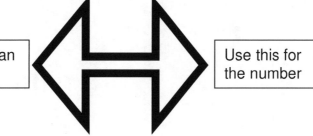

This shape can solve

Use this for the number

(3) 50 ÷ 10 =   90 ÷ 10 =

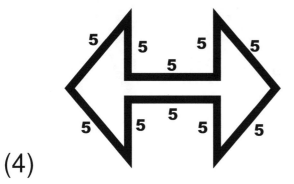
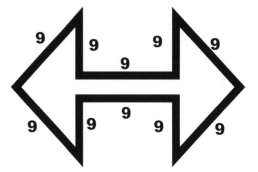

(4)

CHAPTER TEST: MATCHING

Match the number with the shape.

(1) **5**	(A)
(2) **6**	(B)
(3) **10**	(C)
(4) **3**	(D)

CHAPTER TEST: MATCHING

Match the shape with the equation.

(1) 4 x 5 **=**	**(A)**
(2) 3 x 2 **=**	**(B)**

N O T E

Division is the reverse of Multiplication.

Examples:

(1) **6 x 7 = 42**

(2) **4 x 5 = 20**

(1A) **42 ÷ 6 =**

(2A) **20 ÷ 4 =**

GRAPHS

Symbols that aid in showing and representing numbers.

We shall focus on three GRAPH types.

Pie Graph

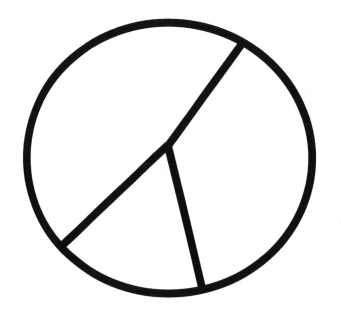

- ☑ Easy to draw
- ☑ Circle shape
- ☑ "Pizza"

Bar Graph

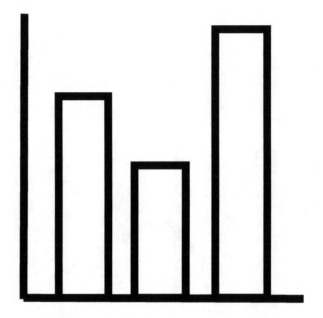

☑ Easy to draw

☑ "Buildings"

Line Graph

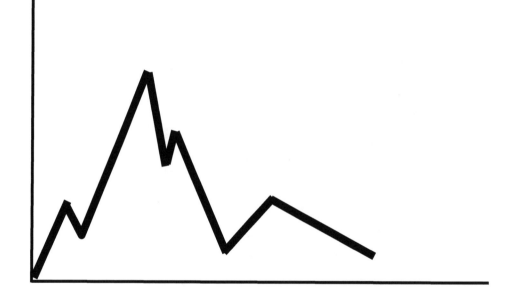

☑ Easy to draw

☑ Show growth / movement

 "Buildings"

GRAPHS
Chapter Test

1. What do Bar graphs look like?
2. What do Pie graphs look like?
3. What do Line graphs show?
4. Draw a Pie graph.
5. Draw a Bar graph.
6. Draw a Line graph.

FRACTIONS in Action

☑ Part(s) of a whole

☑ Piece of something

☑ Paycheck, Pizza

☑ Money, Ice tray

FRACTIONS in Action

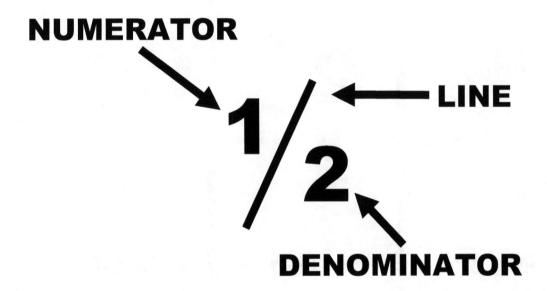

Can you see the differences?

FRACTIONS in Action

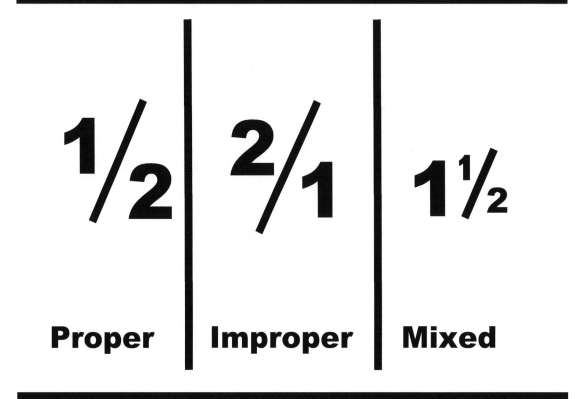

½	2/1	1½
Proper	**Improper**	**Mixed**

Can you see the differences?

FRACTIONS in Action

To Correctly Solve...

- ☑ Denominators must be the same
- ☑ Mixed fractions are fractions, too
- ☑ Follow directions closely
- ☑ Part of our lives.

TERMS to Use

(1) <u>RECIPROCAL</u>

Turn a number upside down.

Ex: 4 = 1/4 -or- 1/2 = 2/1

(2) <u>SIMPLIFY</u>

Divide the top or bottom number by the

highest number exactly.

Ex: 2/4 = 1/2 -or- 5/15 = 1/3

FRACTIONS in Action

Adding <u>Like</u> Denominators

$$2/4 + 1/4 = 3/4$$

(1) Add the numerators together.

(2) Keep the denominator the same

(3) Simplify, if needed

FRACTIONS in Action

Adding <u>Unlike</u> Denominators

$$3/4 + 2/5$$

☑ 4x5 = 20   1) Multiply both denominators

☑ 3x5 = 15   2) Cross-multiply numerators:
                     a) Multiply the 1st numerator

☑ 2x4 = 8   by 2nd denominator
                     b) Multiply the 2nd numerator
                     by 1st denominator

15/20 + 8/20   3) Add the multiplied numerators
                    4) Keep the denominators the
                    same

23/20   ☑ Solve. Simplify, if needed

FRACTIONS in Action

Subtracting <u>Like</u> Denominators

3/4 - 1/4 = 2/4 = 1/2

3-1 = 2	1) Subtract the numerators
4	2) Keep the denominators the same
2/4 = 1/2	☑ Solve. Simplify, if needed

FRACTIONS in Action

Subtracting <u>Unlike</u> Denominators

3/4 - 1/8

4x8 = 32	1) Multiply both denominators

3x8 = 24
1x4 = 4
	2) Cross-multiply numerators:
	  a) Multiply the 1st numerator by 2nd denominator
	  b) Multiply the 2nd numerator by 1st denominator

24/32 – 4/32	3) Add the multiplied numerators 4) Keep the denominators the same
20/32 = 5/8	☑ Solve. Simplify, if needed

FRACTIONS in Action

Multiplying

5/10 x 3/6

5x3 = 15	1) Multiply the numerators
10x6 = 60	2) Multiply the denominators
15/60 = 1/4	☑ Solve. Simplify, if needed

FRACTIONS in Action

Dividing

$5/10 \div 3/6 = 5/10 \times 6/3 = 30/30 = 1$

Do you see when to use the RECIPROCAL?

1) $4/5 \div 3/4 =$

2) $4/5 \times 4/3 =$

3) $16/15$ -or- $1\,1/15$

Can you see how to do it?

FRACTIONS in Action

From Mixed to Improper

(1) Multiply the whole number with the denominator

(2) Add the numerator to the product of step 1.

(3) The answer will be an improper fraction

FRACTIONS in Action

Chapter Test

Make these mixed fractions into improper fractions.

(1) 4 1/4 =

(2) 3 2/3 =

Special Thanks

☑ World Book

☑ My Math Teachers

☑ People who are helped by this book

☑ Math itself, for being so easy!

Printed in the United States
by Baker & Taylor Publisher Services